Merry Christmas!

8 SIMPLE SOLOS FOR THE SEASON
arranged by CAROLYN MILLER ❄ MID-LATER ELEMENTARY

CONTENTS

ISBN 978-1-4584-0803-7

WILLIS MUSIC

EXCLUSIVELY DISTRIBUTED BY

HAL•LEONARD®
CORPORATION
7777 W. BLUEMOUND RD. P.O. BOX 13819 MILWAUKEE, WI 53213

Visit Hal Leonard Online at
www.halleonard.com

Jingle Bells

Words and Music by J. Pierpont
Arranged by Carolyn Miller

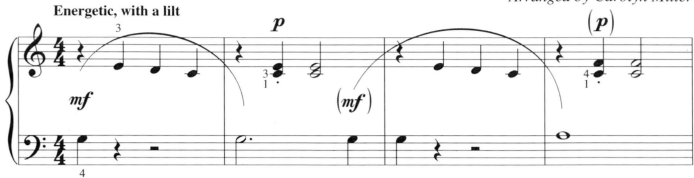

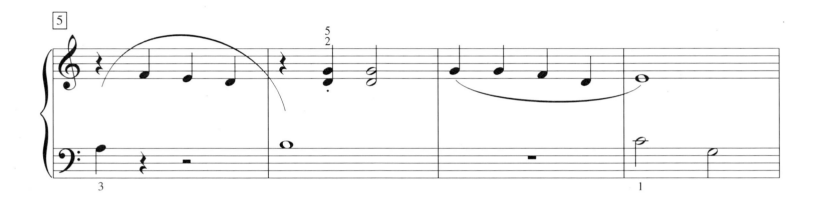

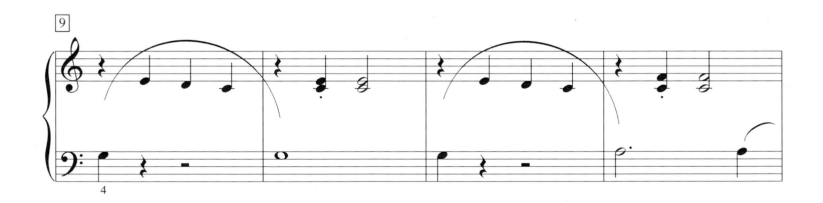

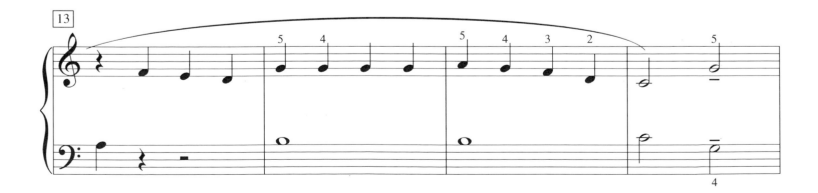

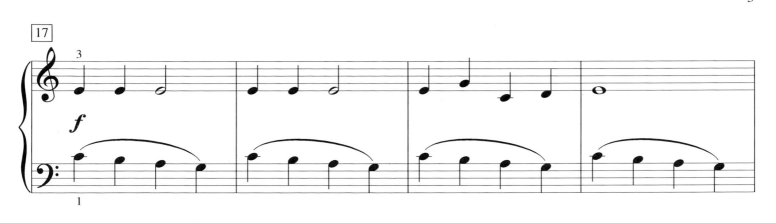

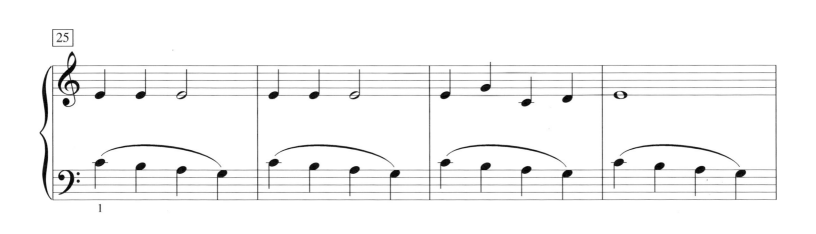

Away in a Manger

Music by James R. Murray
Arranged by Carolyn Miller

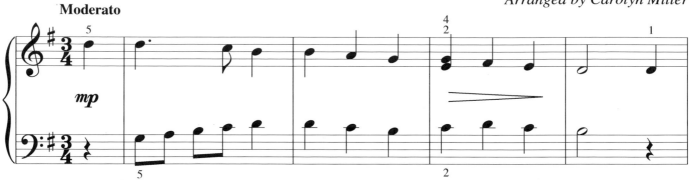

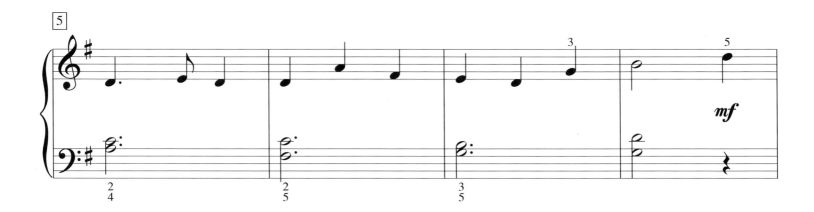

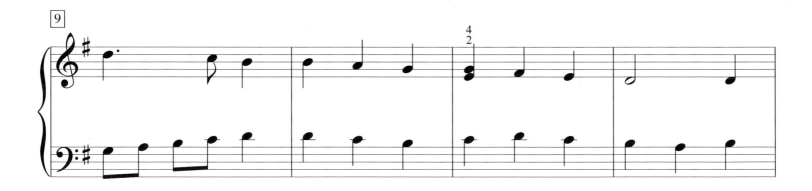

Deck the Hall

Traditional Welsh Carol
Arranged by Carolyn Miller

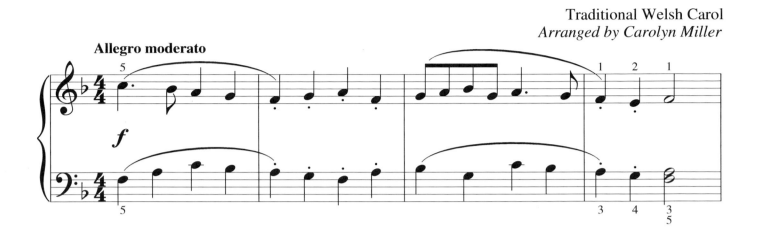

The First Noel

17th Century English Carol
Music from W. Sandys' *Christmas Carols*
Arranged by Carolyn Miller

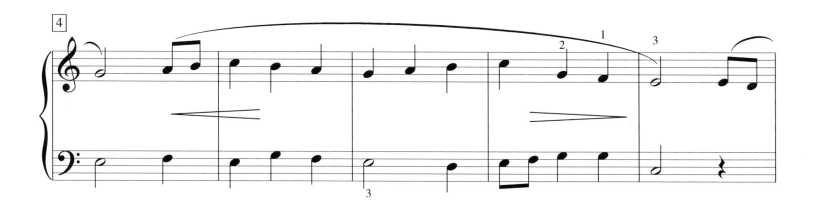

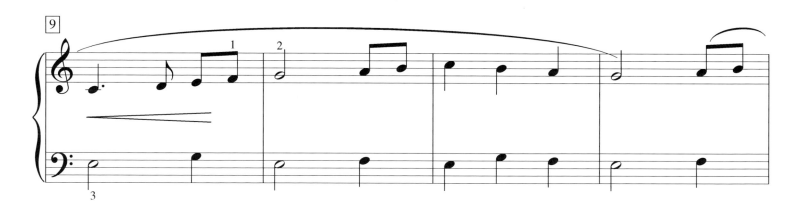

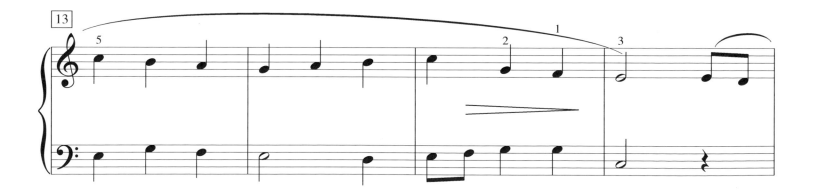

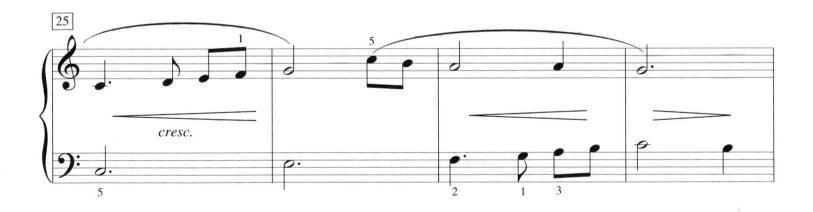

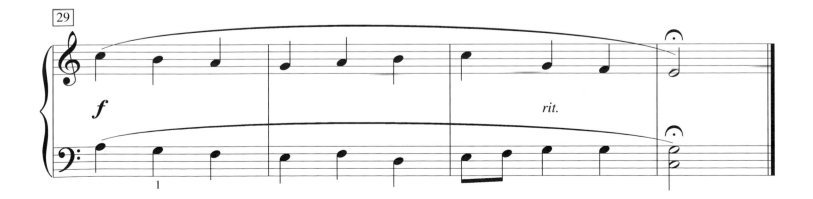

Joy to the World

Words by Isaac Watts
Music by George Frideric Handel
Adapted by Lowell Mason
Arranged by Carolyn Miller

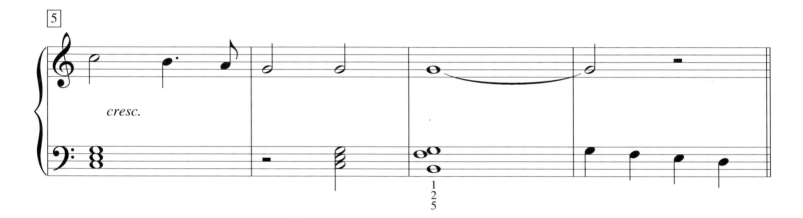

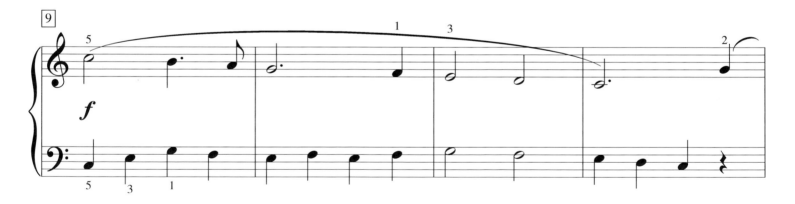

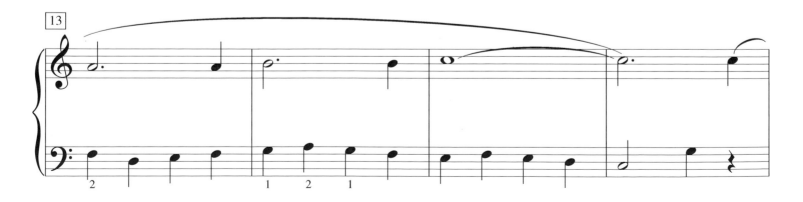

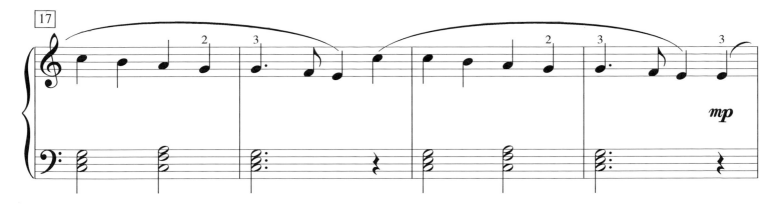

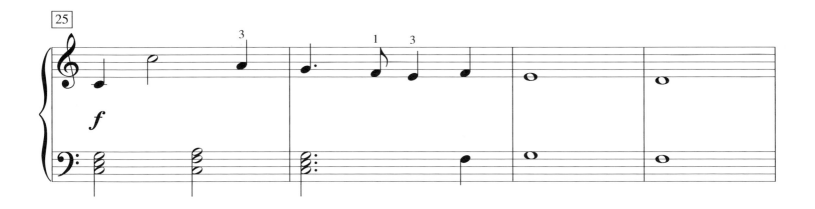

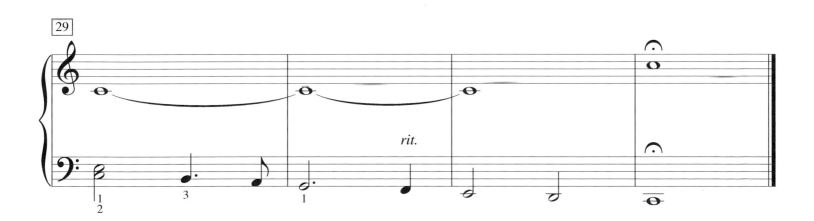

Silent Night

Words by Joseph Mohr
Music by Franz X. Gruber
Arranged by Carolyn Miller

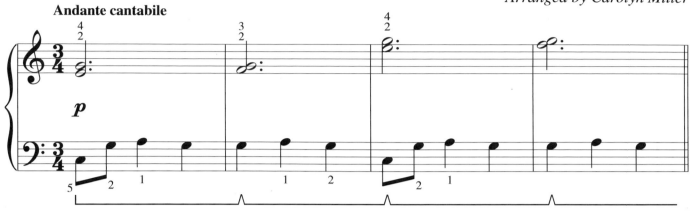

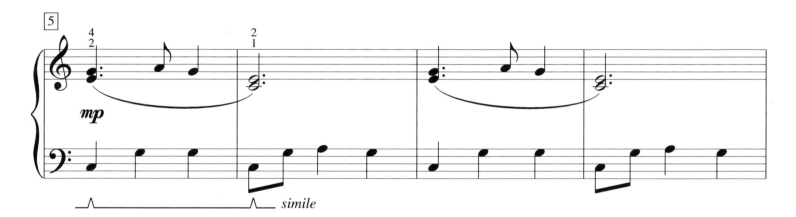

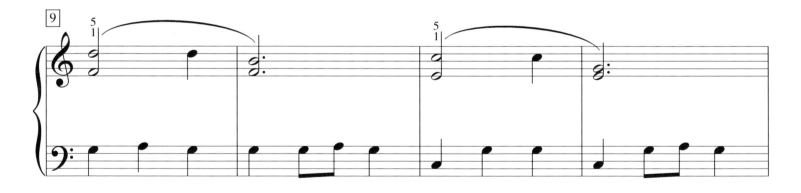

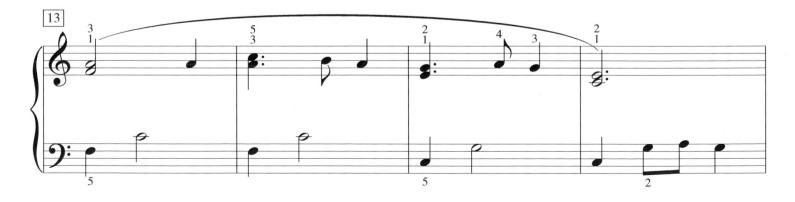

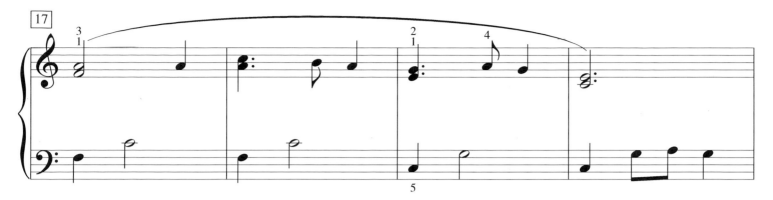

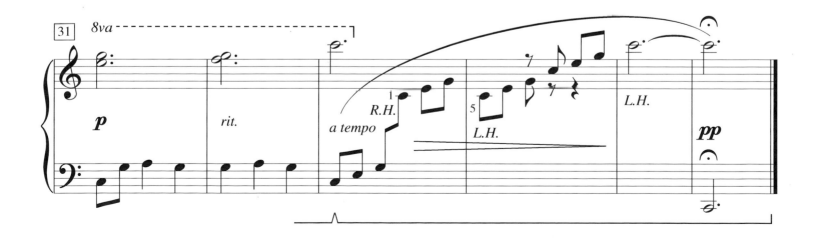

Jolly Old St. Nicholas

Traditional 19th Century American Carol
Arranged by Carolyn Miller

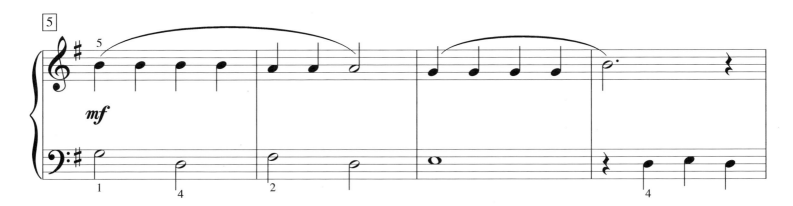

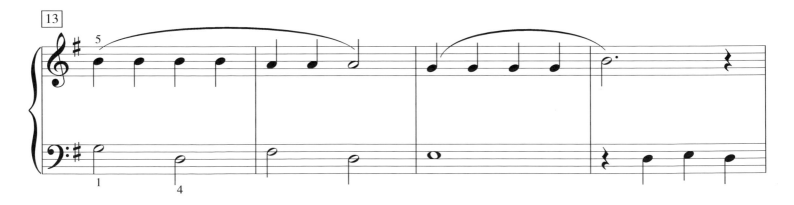

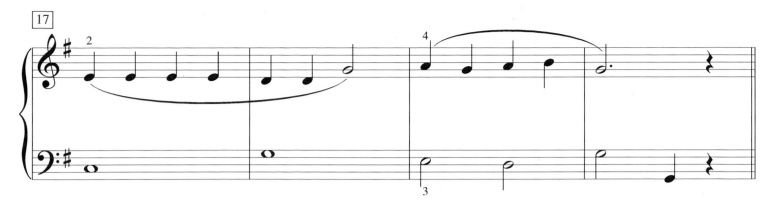

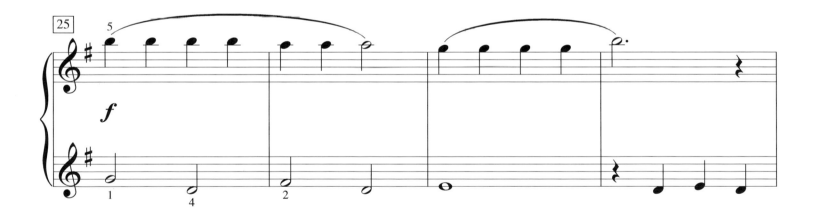

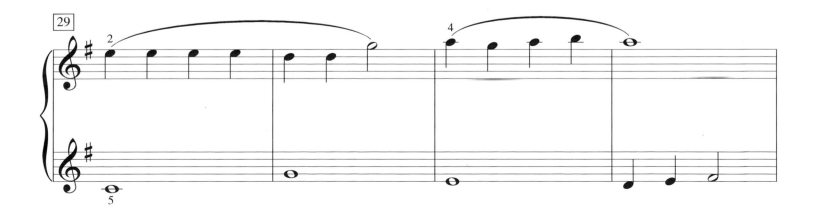

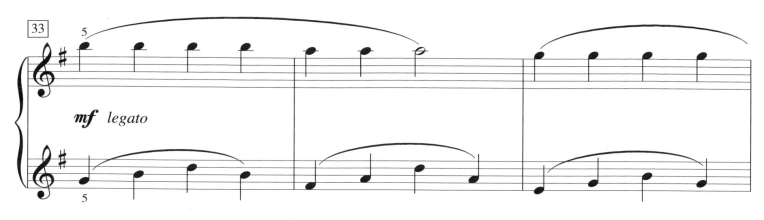

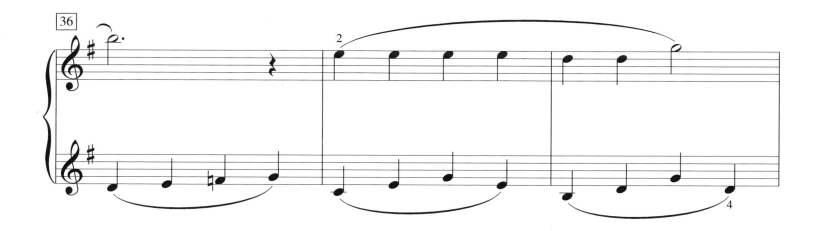

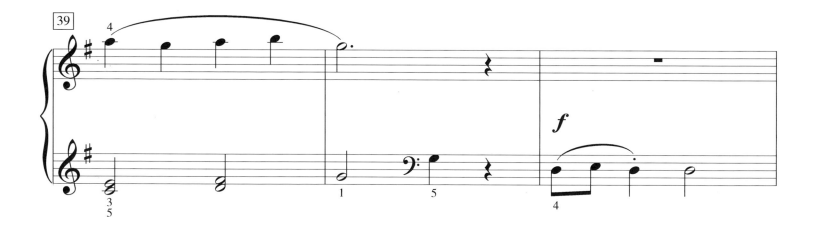